To spend a moment with Morris is to glimpse the secret of life's success. All those experiences so desired by humans are here in the pose of a cat — the warmth, the comfort, attention and fame, the style, grace, and charm. And he does it so easily. Morris simply relaxes with himself.

Capitola Morris photography exhibit statement written by Carolyn Swift, January 1983. This was the first show in Mr. Toots' Coffeehouse featuring Morris photographs by Minna Hertel.

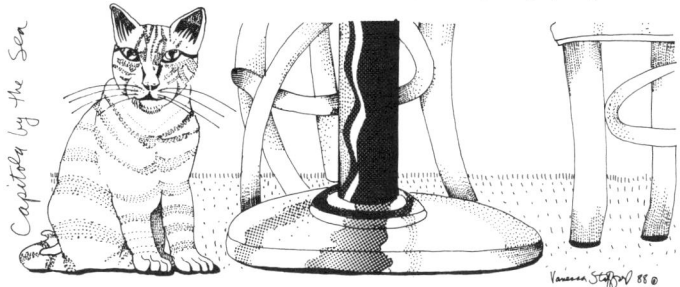

Capitola Morris in Toots', *a coffee cup design by Vanessa Stafford.*

A PHOTOGRAPHIC ESSAY OF A CAPITOLA CAT

Photographs by Minna Hertel

Text by Minna Hertel, Carolyn Swift, and Bob Hansen

Hertel Books
Capitola

Copyright © 1993 Minna Hertel

All rights reserved. No portion of this book may be reproduced or used in any form, or by any means, without prior written permission except for brief use in articles and/or reviews.

For information write:
    Minna Hertel
    210 Esplanade
    Capitola, CA 95010

Book Design/Layout by Minna Hertel

Library of Congress Catalog Card Number: 93-94196

ISBN: 1-881569-01-2

Printed by Color Ad in Monterey, CA
Printed in the United States of America

First edition
10 9 8 7 6 5 4 3 2 1 0

Photograph Acknowledgments
Page 10 Ron Ruffner and Morris
Page 26 Clare Hertel and Morris
Page 36 Capitola Mayor Ron Graves
            and Morris
Page 45 Artist Rick Stroup and Morris
Page 57 Photographer Minna Hertel
            and Morris

Grateful acknowledgment is given to the *Santa Cruz Sentinel* for permission to reprint "The cat with a mistaken identity borrows a life" on page 6.

Acknowledgments

So many people knew and loved Capitola Morris I thought it was important to tell his life story with pictures. He inspired poets to compose poetry, authors to write, artists to draw, and me to photograph. Unaffected, in his cat way, he lived his life in simple dignity doing the things he liked to do. He chose to live on the Esplanade. He picked me to be his main human. And Mr. Toots' was where he chose to hang out. He was not "our cat"; we were "his people."

I want to thank those who gave permission to use their work or image in this book. At the top of the list is Bob Hansen, who was the "voice" of Morris in the Mr. Toots' Newsletter ("Morris Column" 1983-1984), and he was there for Morris when help from a human was needed, for love, food, and medical care. A special thanks goes to Carolyn Swift for writing the exhibit statements for my photography shows in Mr. Toots' featuring Morris. Also Vanessa Stafford for permission to use her drawing of Morris sitting on the floor of Mr. Toots'. Thank you, Coeleen Kiebert for your support and help with this book.

And a thank-you to my mother, Ann L. Hertel and my brother, Herbert Hertel, who fed Morris whenever I was away. Also, deep appreciation and thanks to all who loved and cared for a Capitola cat known as Morris of the Esplanade.

Minna Hertel

Introduction
◆By Carolyn Swift, from the 1985 Photography Exhibit

This is a mouser so extra ordinary he has collected numerous names— all typical cat titles that suit his standard frame, tawny color, and placid nature. No more lissome, lethargic customer ever climbed the stairs at Mr. Toots' Coffeehouse, or blended in quite so well.

Known here as "Morris," he often catches the unwary patron by surprise. Camouflaged on the rust-colored rug, he gingerly winds through a forest of ankles. Affecting mild catalepsy, he sometimes is mistaken for a sofa cushion. Or he is more loosely unfurled before the heater, a paw over an ear in a pose that suggests a hangover. (Indeed, Morris does have nocturnal hangouts— the River's End, the Edgewater, and the Capitola Hotel.)

Aloof and affable Morris is the epitome of "Capitola casual" and evidence of the saying, "Cats will always lie soft." While out-of-doors, he pussyfoots on the rooftops and dabs in nature's sandbox on the beach, but his passion is always the angles of repose. Tourists and locals alike know Morris best as "that tomcat that's been sleeping on my car." He favors well-waxed front-engine models, and any make will do. To some folks, the orange ball against the windshield is a nuisance. To those of us who know and love Morris, however, it is an honor to find he has graced our hoods with his feline inertia.

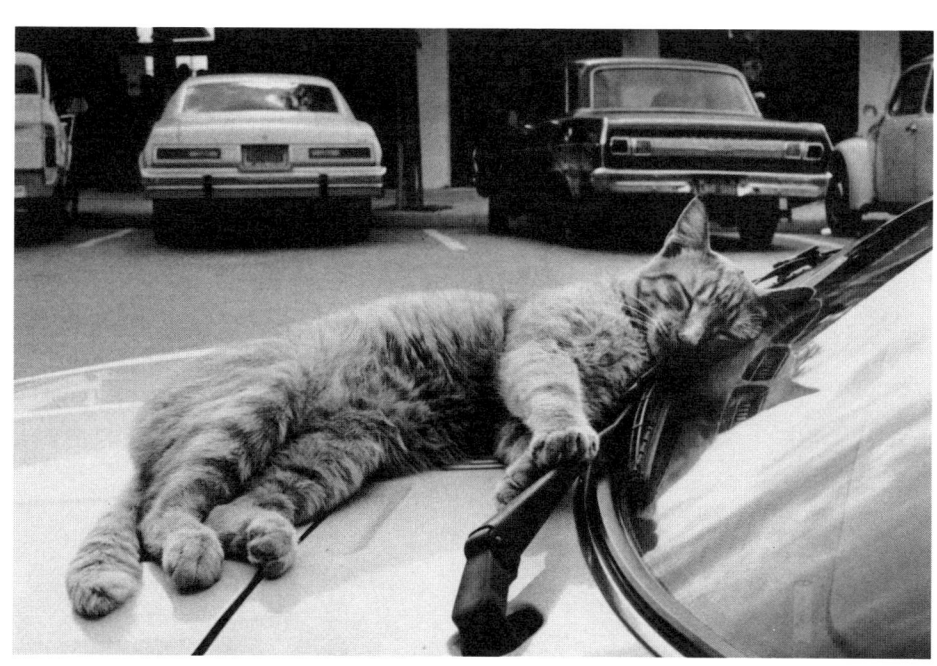

Prologue

◆By Minna Hertel

There was once a tabby cat who lived on the Esplanade in Capitola-by-the-Sea. No one really knew just when he first appeared or where he had come from. One day he was simply there, and a part of our lives. Eventually everyone who came in contact with this enchanting cat had a special story to tell about the encounter. He had become famous in the territory he had claimed.

In the beginning he was a cat with many names. At the Edgewater Restaurant he was called "Roscoe." The boatman of the Lagoon called him "Capitola Tom." A soft-sculpture artist next door called him "Tommy." A waitress in the coffeehouse called him "Maurice." His main human called him "Rusty." Everyone else called him "Morris" because of his resemblance to the famous 9-Lives cat. As the years passed, the moniker "Morris" became the name locals and tourists, and even Morris himself, came to accept. In 1983 his fame and name were documented in the *Santa Cruz Sentinel*, "Morris, the famous Capitola Village cat."

A-16—Santa Cruz Sentinel — Sunday, Oct. 23, 1983

The cat with a mistaken identity borrows a life

CAPITOLA — They say cats have nine lives, but a stray orange tabby had to borrow one — from Morris, the famous Capitola Village cat.

It was a true case of mistaken identity.

The folks at Santa Cruz Veterinary Hospital operated on the fractured shoulder of a cat brought in by an Animal Shelter employee, thinking it was Morris. Morris, who can often be found hanging around Mr. Toot's Restaurant, is known throughout the Village. The Morris look-alike was found injured in the Village.

Surgery nurse Penny Robertson called Bob Hansen, owner of Mr. Toot's, and asked if Morris was missing. He said Morris indeed was missing. The hospital offered to do the $400 operation for free, because, as Robertson said, "we all knew and loved Morris."

It was only after Dr. James Roush finished the surgery, that who would be seen walking around town, but Morris.

Today, the Morris look-alike is doing fine, resting comfortably at the hospital. The real Morris is back to sipping warm milk at Mr. Toot's.

"It's just kind of funny. We did a free surgery on someone's cat," said Robertson, who only wants to find the rightful owner.

Reprinted with permission of the *Santa Cruz Sentinel*.

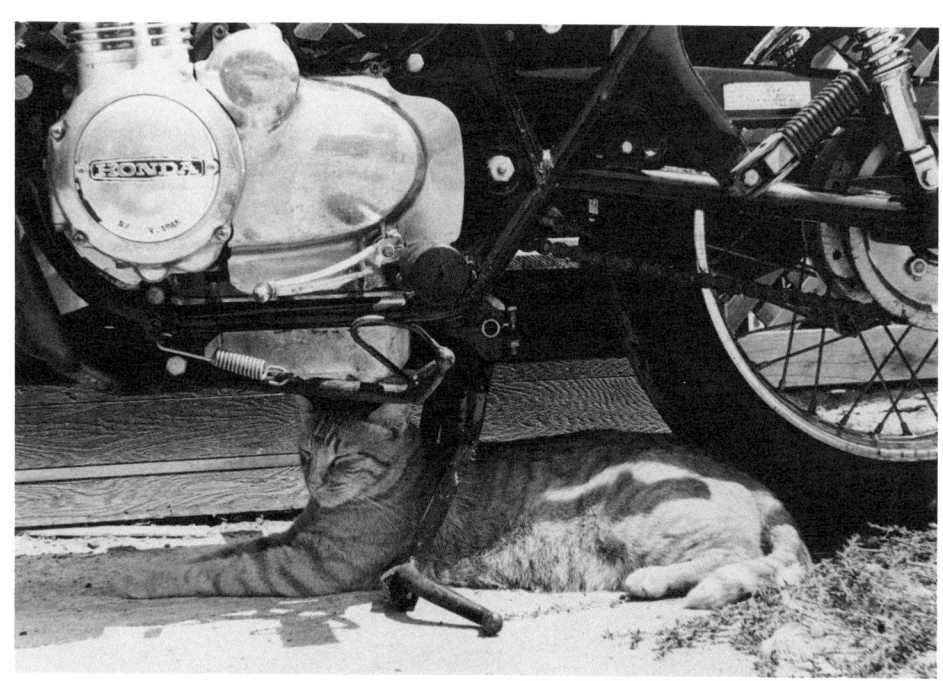

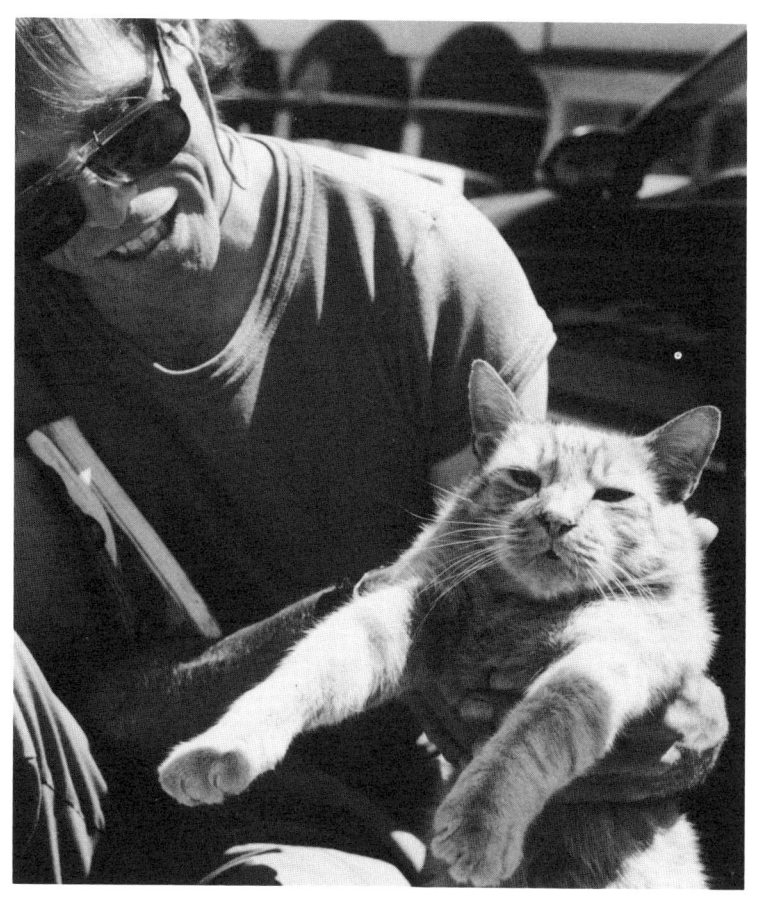

A photographic collague created with photographs of Capitola Morris set around a photograph of the graffiti blackboard in Mr. Toots' (1988). The comments were written by coffeehouse customers.

Epilogue

◆By Bob Hansen, from the Mr. Toots' menu Summer 1992

Mr. Toots opened for business in February 1978. I remember that it was slow that first year. Often there would be more cats in the room than customers. Of course I did my best to throw the cats out as soon as they came in, and that discouraged most of them from coming back, but there was one cat, an orange tabby who resembled the one in the cat food commercials on t.v., who simply wouldn't take the hint. Again and again I'd throw him out the front door and in less than a minute he'd be in again through the same door. In time, I gave it up, and Mr. Toots was Morris's home for several years (1978-1991). Anyone will tell you that Morris was the one who really owned the place. I think he also owned every other establishment on the Esplanade as well, and no one would have been surprised if he had gotten himself elected to the city council. He was that kind of a cat.

But the years caught up with Morris. He slowed down considerably and everyone was worried he'd fall asleep in the street some day and be hit by a car. Finally, Minna Hertel, who loves Morris as much as I do, bundled him up about a year ago and took him home with her to finish out his days more safely in Aptos. He adapted easily to the change, but his health did not improve. Minna phoned today and reported that he's sick and at the vet's for examination and that it doesn't look good. You silly old cat, Morris, why can't you live forever? That's what I want to know.

Capitola Morris and his main human, photographer Minna Hertel, on the Esplanade in Capitola Village (1986).